Creative Kids

MAKE YOUR OWN NEWSPAPER

By
Chris & Ray Harris

♦

Art & Design
Don Brunelle

Featuring
Newsnose
the
Newshound
Ace Reporter

A Newspower® Production

This book and newspaper kit is available at special quantity discounts
for bulk purchases. For information, contact the publisher at
1-800-872-5627.

Published by Bob Adams, Inc.
260 Center Street, Holbrook, Massachusetts 02343

Manufactured in the United States of America.

A B C D E F G H I J

ISBN: 1-55850-219-X

Contents

Getting Started
Why Everybody Loves to Make a Newspaper!

Want to get someone's attention? Just ask, *"Have you heard the latest?"* It's the one conversation-starter that's sure to make your audience sit up and take notice!

Heard what? Heard who won the game? Heard what happened in school yesterday? Heard about the new kid? Heard about the hurricane? People want to know what's happening. That's why they read newspapers and watch television newscasts. Few things are as exciting—or as important—as the news.

There's news being made around the clock and around the world. But the news we turn to first is the news closest to home: news about family, friends, school, and our own town. Editors of hometown newspapers pick and choose the news their readers want to know. When you make your own newspaper, *you're* the editor, and *you* choose the news that's important to you and your readers. That's the thrill—and the responsibility—of being a newspaper reporter and editor.

Five Different Newspaper Sections or One Big Newspaper!

Look through your favorite local newspaper and you'll find different parts, or sections—a travel section, for instance, or a sports section, or a book and movie review section.

Your *Make-Your-Own Newspaper* has five different sections: a main section with news and comics; a section for your opinions, leisure activities, and advertisements; a book and movie review section, a travel section, and a sports section. You can make five different kinds of newspapers at different times. Or you can make one big, 20-page newspaper by putting all the sections inside one another.

However you do it, your Make-Your-Own Newspapers are ready for you to fill up with your own news and pictures. All you need is your imagination, a nose for news, a pencil, and some coloring crayons or markers. The result will be a real newspaper that you can proudly share with your readers.

YOUR READERS! These are great words. It means that others are reading your ideas—and hearing what you have to say. It means you are making waves in the world. You are important. People are taking notice of you.

It's Easy to Make Your Own Newspaper!

1. Get out Section A of THE REPORTER.

Notice that the top of your newspaper looks like this:

The blank line is important. It lets you give a special name to your newspaper. For example, if your name is Jones, you may want to call your newspaper *THE JONES FAMILY REPORTER,* or *THE CHRIS JONES REPORTER,* using your own name. You can use the name of your school, your town, your neighborhood, or any other name you can think of. You may think of a name like *THE CRUSADING REPORTER, or THE INVESTIGATIVE REPORTER.*

There is another space that says EDITED BY: _____ .

That's you. You are the editor-in-chief, so write your name in this space. If you are making the newspaper with a friend, put both your names in the space. Then add the date of your newspaper.

2. You don't need a computer or typewriter for this newspaper. You can write your stories and articles directly onto the page of your newspaper with a good dark pencil, or a pen.

3. Newspaper reporters always write a rough copy of their stories first, before putting them into the newspaper. This is called a rough draft. You will want to do the same.

   Write your rough draft on a separate piece of paper. Correct your story and make changes to be sure it is exactly the way you want it. Then copy the story into your newspaper. All good reporters work this way.

If you want to use a computer or typewriter, print your articles in columns the same width as the Make-Your-Own Newspaper columns. Then cut the articles out and paste them onto your newspaper pages.

4. You can make pictures to go with your stories and articles in one of these ways: Draw a picture yourself in the picture boxes provided for you. Then color it. Or, find a good picture in a newspaper or magazine. Cut it out and paste it in the picture box of your newspaper.

You may find a photo around the house that you can use. Or, take a picture with a camera. A Polaroid-type camera, if you have one, will give you an instant picture. Paste the picture in the picture box.

5. The best-looking newspapers have lots of color. Color any parts of your newspaper you think will look good in color. Use crayons, colored pencils, or colored markers. If you use markers, use the kind that don't soak through the paper. ***Try your marker first on a corner of the newspaper before you use it.*** Some markers that are too wet soak through the paper and mess up the other side.

THE REPORTER
Section A

News • Weather
What's Happening
Exclusive Interview
Comics
Fun Features

The Front Page

NEWS FLASH

If someone asks you, "What happened in school today?" you might say, "Oh, nothing." Lots of things happened, you mean, but nothing *unusual* happened. No breaking news, in other words. You went to classes, had lunch, met and talked with people, played basketball, maybe. But if there had been a fire in the boiler room, if the local slam-dunk expert had pulled down the basketball hoop, and if a teacher had jumped out of the window, then you would have *news* to report.

The first page of a newspaper always contains a *lead* story. This is the story the newspaper editor thinks will get the most attention from most readers. So the story you write for the front page of *Section A* of the Make-Your-Own Newspaper will be your lead story—the story you think will do most

to grab and hold your readers. A news story always starts with a headline that tells in a few words what the story is about. A good headline will make a reader want to read the story. The box under the words *NEWS FLASH!* is for your headline.

News stories give readers some basic facts: **who**, **what**, **where**, **when**, **why** and **how**. Say, for example, your front page story is about a science field trip to sample water quality at different points along a nearby river.

Here's how your story might turn out...

STUDENTS MONITOR RIVER WATER
By Linda Healy

(who) Fourteen members of Mr. Miles' 10th grade science class . . . *(what)* participated in a field trip . . . *(when)* on Saturday, April 22nd . . . *(why)* to monitor water quality . . . *(where)* at six locations along the Connecticut River between Brattleboro and Turners Falls . . . *(how)* The students used canoes to travel from one spot to the next, filling and labeling test tubes with water taken from each site.

This is a complete news story as it stands. But you can add meaning to your story by answering two more questions: What is the background? and, So what?

By background we mean what led up to this story. Why, in this case, is it necessary to check the quality of the river water? The second question is, "So what?" In other words, why does it matter to the reader?

By answering these last two questions, your story might end like this:

(background) Factories along the Connecticut have agreed to clean up waste water before discharging it into the river. . . *(so what?)* Regular testing of water quality will help keep the Connecticut River clean, safe and beautiful.

Illustrating Your Story and Writing a Caption

The picture box next to the story provides a place to illustrate your story. You can create pictures in many ways. You can draw your own picture and color it using pastels, crayons or colored pencils. If you use felt-tip markers, *test one first* in a corner to make sure it doesn't bleed through the paper and make a mess on the other side. You can cut out pictures you find in a newspaper, in magazines, on calendars, post cards, and so on, and paste them in place in the picture box. A colorful picture adds eye-appeal to your newspaper.

Again, don't overlook the option of taking your own photographs to illustrate your story. That way, you get just the picture you want! A Polaroid-type camera will give you an instant picture.

When you have your picture in place, write a caption below it. A caption is a few words that tell something about what's going on. If there are people in the picture, you should give their names. If the place is important, you should identify the scene. If the picture emphasizes a point made in the news story, you should explain how the picture relates to the story.

The Weather Vane

The weather is always news—it lands on us all, and it's a part of our world we cannot control. But there's more to weather than just today's temperature. Your weather box can offer many kinds of weather news, which you can pick up from televised forecasts, from the weather section in your daily newspaper, or from your own weather-recording instruments. For example:

Highs and Lows: What was the highest temperature recorded in the past 24 hours, or in the past week? What was the lowest? What is the average temperature for this date?

Weather Trends: Will it get warmer in the next few days, or colder? Wetter or dryer? And then there's lifestyle advice: what to wear, forecasts for outdoor activities and events, and health alerts such as smog, frostbite, windchill, or heat stroke warnings.

Choosing one or two of these weather-related items will add depth to your weather report.

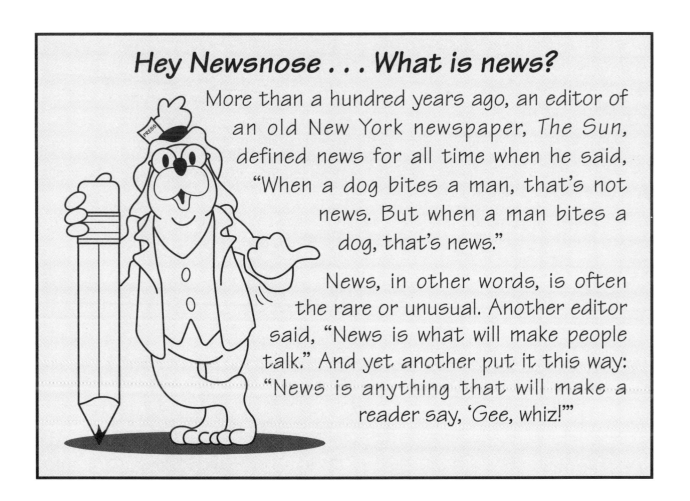

Hey Newsnose ... What is news?

More than a hundred years ago, an editor of an old New York newspaper, *The Sun,* defined news for all time when he said, "When a dog bites a man, that's not news. But when a man bites a dog, that's news."

News, in other words, is often the rare or unusual. Another editor said, "News is what will make people talk." And yet another put it this way: "News is anything that will make a reader say, 'Gee, whiz!'"

What's Happening

AROUND SCHOOL, AROUND TOWN, and AROUND THE WORLD

News happens everywhere. All you have to do is watch for it. Keep your eyes, ears, and imagination wide open. Your imagination is important because it helps you sense where a story exists. Some reporters call this "having a nose for news."

Start with the "Around School" column. Ask yourself—"What's happening that other people will want to know about?" Awards and honors always make it into the newspapers. A new principal or new teacher will make a difference to a lot of people. Shows, contests, and field trips are always interesting for others to read about.

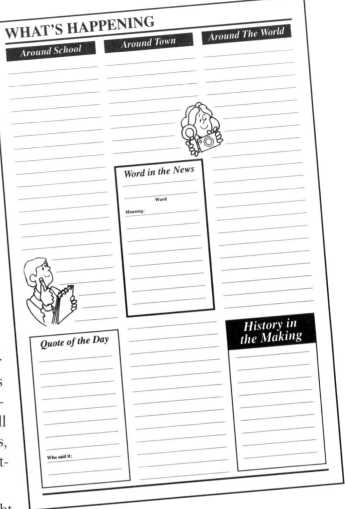

In the "Around Town" column you might want to talk about what you and your friends are doing outside of school. Got a project going? What is it? Where do you hang out and why? Read your local newspaper, check the radio and watch your local TV news to find out what's happening in your neighborhood.

There might be a big weather story if there has just been a storm. Crimes, fires, and accidents are news. If you want an exciting experience, stop by the nearest police or fire station and tell the officer on duty you're looking for a story for your newspaper.

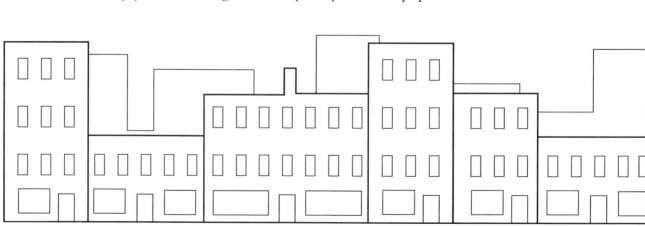

You will have to get your "Around the World" story from other news sources: newspapers, news magazines, and television. If you have done some world traveling yourself, tell about that. Or, you may have learned something in school about what's going on in the world that will be interesting for your readers.

QUOTES, WORD IN THE NEWS, and HISTORY IN THE MAKING

These kinds of short articles are sometimes called fillers. A filler is a short article that is used by a newspaper to fill up a little bit of empty space on a page. These can be a bit of serious stuff, a did-you-know fun fact, a joke, a quotation, or anything else you can think of that can be told in a few words.

There are three fillers on the "What's Happening" page of your newspaper. One is a quote of the day. Keep your ears open. Did one of your friends or a relative say something funny? Interesting? Unusual? Is there a quote you heard or read about in history that you really like? Maybe there was a funny one-liner on your favorite TV show that others would enjoy.

Another filler is a "Word in the News." Words are interesting. People like to find out about new words so that they can use them themselves. Find a long word, a strange word, a funny word, a foreign word. Look the word up in a dictionary if you have to. Then use your own words to explain what it means.

The last filler item on the "What's Happening" page is "History in the Making." Today's news is tomorrow's history. Once again, you can pick an important event from your local newspaper. Is there a battle somewhere? It may be in the history books your children will use. What has your local representative in government done lately? Was a new baby born in your family? That baby may be a world leader forty years from now. It's all history in the making.

Dear Newsnose . . . What's a by-line?

A by-line is just what it sounds like: a line telling who the story is by—who wrote the story. The by-line appears after the headline. Not every news story carries a by-line, and not every by-line is a person's name. Sometimes the by-line will read Staff. That means more than one reporter at the newspaper contributed to the story.

Sometimes the by-line says The Associated Press or gives the name of some other organization. This means the story came from a news service that covers news around the world and sells its stories to many newspapers. Most by-lines, of course give the name of a reporter. In this case, that's you!

Person to Person

FEATURING . . . *and* PERSONAL PROFILE

The Person to Person page of your newspaper combines an interview with a personal profile. An interview is one of the toughest jobs for a reporter. It's not always easy to face another person eyeball to eyeball and ask personal questions. But it is one of the most interesting jobs you will do.

There are all kinds of people to interview. You will find that plain, everyday people are very interesting once you talk to them and start asking questions.

Here are just a few of the people you can think of to interview:

- *Friends* • *Family members* • *Teachers*
- *Fire fighters* • *Police officers*
- *Senior citizens* • *Coaches*
- *Veterans* • *Farmers*

To make interviewing easier, prepare a list of questions ahead of time that you want to ask. You don't always know where the answers to the questions will lead, but they break the ice and get you started.

The Person to Person page has six questions to get an interview started. Make notes as you ask your questions. If you have a tape recorder to record your subject's answers, use that.

If the questions that are written on the Person to Person page don't work for the person you are interviewing, make up your own questions. Here are some other questions you can use:

An older person
"What was school like when you were young?"

Farmer
"What do you raise on your farm?"

Police officer
"What is the hardest part of your job?"

Anyone
"Tell me about your work."

The Personal Profile column provides a quick look at your subject. It gives a first impression of a person, while the interview goes into more detail.

Hey Newsnose! What's an "exclusive" and what's a "personal profile"?

An "exclusive" is a story written just by you for your newspaper. No other newspaper has the story.

A "profile" can be a view of the side of your head. The man who is sitting down at the top of the Person-to-Person page, for example, has his head shown in "profile." But a written profile is a description of a person in words. A person's age, as well as a little about the person's family, likes, and dislikes can all go into a profile.

The Fun Page

COMICS

There are two comic strips on your fun page. The first one sets up a funny situation and leaves it up to you to write the punch line—the gag line. What strategy would a coach have for the second half of a game when his team is behind 86 to 0? Hide? Call his mother for help?

The second strip is blank. This allows you to create a whole comic of your own. Or, you can cut a favorite comic from your local newspaper and paste it in place. Color your comics to make them more eye catching.

I PREDICT

Your prediction for the future can be funny or serious:

I predict that more women will be national leaders in the future.

I predict that I will be the first person to land on Mars.

I predict that homework will be abolished forever.

WOULD YOU BELIEVE . . .

"Would you believe . . ." is a place for an interesting fact:

Would you believe a meteorite measuring six miles across was discovered in Mexico? It hit the earth 65 million years ago and may have led to the extinction of the dinosaurs.

Would you believe that China is a country with more than a billion people?

You can find many interesting facts in encyclopedias, in a sports almanac, or in newspapers and magazines. You may even be able to pluck a fun fact from your own store of knowledge.

What can you predict in the "I predict" box? You can foretell just about anything you want to about the future. Your prediction can be funny or serious. It can be who you think will win the next election, or what you think you will be doing ten years from now:

"I predict the Chicago Cubs will win the pennant in the year 2050."

"I predict I will become a world famous underwater tuba player."

BLANK WORD BALLOONS

The two people with empty word balloons are waiting for you to give them something to say:

"I've been appointed assistant band leader."
"I guess that makes you a band aid!"

WORD SCRAMBLE

You probably know how a word scramble works. Find a word in your dictionary that has seven or eight letters. The object is to see how many words can be made using letters you select from the letters of the long word.

Dear Newsnose:
Why are comics called "comics" when they're not always funny?

When comics first appeared in newspapers in the early 1900's, they were always funny. Some people still call them "the funnies" or "the funny papers."

Little by little, more serious subjects began to appear—"Superman," "Mary Worth," "Prince Valiant," "Mark Trail" and others.

But the names "comics" and "funnies" stuck, and everything that is in cartoon strip form is referred to in this way.

THE REPORTER
Section B

Editorial • Editorial Cartoon
Reporter Poll • Meetings
Movies and Television
Music
Advertising

Editorial Page

THE EDITORIAL

Look at the editorial pages of your local newspaper. They are easy to recognize. There are one or more columns that give opinions on various issues, a political cartoon, and sometimes letters to the editor from newspaper readers.

An editorial column might discuss some very heavy problems, such as going to war, or it might just be about school lunches (say, the value of hot dogs and sauerkraut as opposed to a salad bar).

While you are reading the editorials in your local newspaper, look at the cartoons that are nearby. Editorial cartoons are funny pictures with a message that may be important. They also express the opinions and feelings of the cartoonist toward a special problem. The drawing is an editorial in picture form, in other words.

The editorial in the newspaper you are making is set up so that you can start by telling your readers what problem you are writing about. Next, explain why this problem is important. Then, tell what you think should be done about the problem.

THE EDITORIAL CARTOON

After you have written your editorial, draw an editorial cartoon. This cartoon should help your readers understand how you feel about the problem you have chosen to talk about. If the problem is one that has been discussed in newspapers and magazines, you may be able to find a cartoon to cut out and paste in the box instead of drawing one of your own.

THE REPORTER POLL

A poll (pronounced "pole") is a survey that tells how people feel about a subject. Is three hours of homework a day enough or too much? Should schools charge kids a fee for playing sports?

When you take a poll, write down a question or statement that people can reply yes or no to—agree or disagree. For example:

Do you agree or disagree with the following statement?

A fee should be charged for playing school sports.

Teachers should require three hours of homework each day.

When you have decided on the question you want to ask, find some people and start asking. Keep track of all the yes and no responses on a piece of paper. After you have talked to ten people (or more if you are feeling ambitious), count up the results and write your story.

Hold it please, Newsnose! What's an editorial?

When you read the first part of the word editorial—editor—you've got it. An editorial is the opinion of an editor of the newspaper about an issue or a problem. Since you are the editor of the newspaper, it is up to you to think of a problem you want to sound off about and—well, sound off.

The Leisure Page

MEETINGS – EVENTS

In the meetings and events section you can tell about one important event in detail, or you can list a number of happenings telling just the date, time, and place. If you don't know where to start, try your own busy schedule for the week: an important game, band practice, karate, or gymnastics.

DON'T MISS!

At the bottom of the page there's a "Don't Miss" box where you can tell about a really special event you think your readers shouldn't miss—a camping trip, a shopping spree in the city, a homecoming rally. You can even make something up : Next Tuesday evening, Dr. Zgltyl—a visitor from Mars—will be speaking about space travel from the roof of his flying saucer.

THE MINI REVIEW

The mini-review can tell about a movie, a book, a play, or a television program. You will want to give your readers more than your opinion: GREAT! or IT STINKS! You should start off a review with some facts about the book or show you are reviewing: Who's in it? What's it about?

Then, your opinion—good or bad—should be backed up by a reason. Was the acting good or bad? Was the story exciting or boring? True to life or not believable? Did it make you laugh? Was it supposed to be funny, but wasn't?

FOUR STAR SNACK

No leisure page is complete without an article about food. That's because most people spend about half their leisure time eating.

Everybody has a favorite snack. This is the place to tell the world about it. Tell how to make it if it's a little snack. But if your idea of a favorite snack is a turkey dinner, just list the food and skip how to make it.

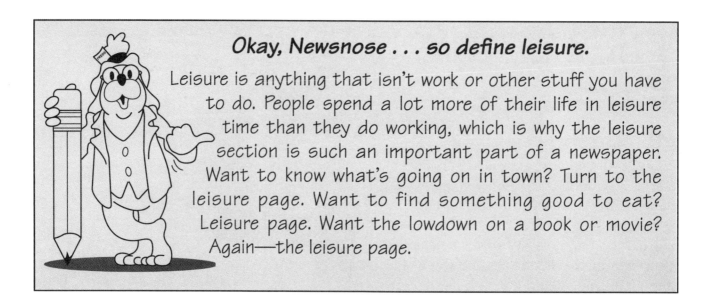

Okay, Newsnose . . . so define leisure.

Leisure is anything that isn't work or other stuff you have to do. People spend a lot more of their life in leisure time than they do working, which is why the leisure section is such an important part of a newspaper. Want to know what's going on in town? Turn to the leisure page. Want to find something good to eat? Leisure page. Want the lowdown on a book or movie? Again—the leisure page.

The Music Page

GREAT SOUNDS AROUND

There are great sounds around everywhere. Pick the kind of music you like and know best, and tell your friends, the readers, all about it.

The music topic that newspaper reporters write about most often is new releases. If you have heard a new song or a new album, describe it for your readers and tell them your opinion of it.

You will have more to talk about if you can find out something about the lyrics, the instruments that are played, and who plays them. You may find this information on album covers or in news about new releases in newspapers and music magazines.

But you don't have to talk about the music other people make if you are a musician yourself. Write an article about the instrument you play, about the music you like to play best, and about experiences you may have playing with other musicians.

An article about a certain kind of music can also be interesting for your readers. A story about the beginnings of rock and roll, or about where jazz came from, would make great stories.

COMING ON STRONG

This column gives you a chance to talk about something new you have discovered in music. It may be a musical event—a group coming to town, or a performance by a solo musician.

Perhaps you have heard a new kind of music you haven't been aware of before. Describe it for your readers and tell why you like it. You may hear a single on the radio that isn't popular yet, but that is so good you can predict it will soon appear high on the charts. Your readers will want to share your discovery.

TEN BEST

There are at least three ways you can fill in this chart. One, find the top-ten chart on the entertainment page of your newspaper and copy it. Two, get the opinions of a group of your friends and make a list of favorite music this way. Three, just make a list of your own all-time favorites.

A WORD ABOUT MUSIC

Think of a word or expression from the world of music that is strange or interesting. Write it down and then explain it for your readers. If you are into rap, it would be fun to explain the words hip hop, wack, and dope. Tell what reggae is, or define soul, or ragtime. You would be surprised how many of your readers would like the real lowdown on musical terms they hear all the time but don't really understand.

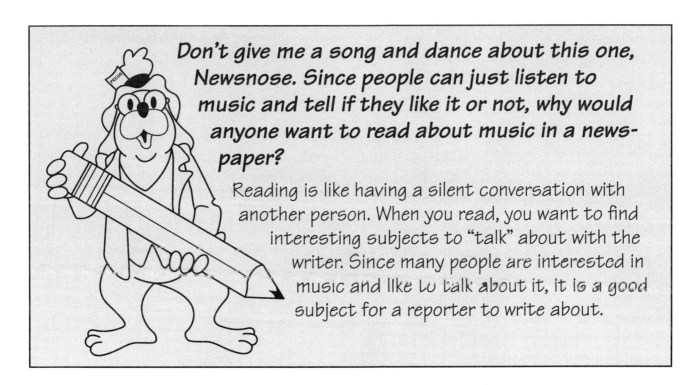

Don't give me a song and dance about this one, Newsnose. Since people can just listen to music and tell if they like it or not, why would anyone want to read about music in a newspaper?

Reading is like having a silent conversation with another person. When you read, you want to find interesting subjects to "talk" about with the writer. Since many people are interested in music and like to talk about it, it is a good subject for a reporter to write about.

Classified Ads

WRITING ADS

People are always losing things and finding things. Folks feel so badly about losing a pet or a valuable ring or a wallet, that newspapers like to help as a service to their readers.

People use job wanted classified ads (also called situation wanted ads) when they're looking for work, and they use help wanted ads when they're looking for a worker to hire.

When you write a job wanted ad, be sure to make yourself sound like an employer just can't do without you. Tell exactly what you want to work at. Tell about your experience and how reliable you are. Don't beg for work. Instead, make people want to hire you because you sound like you can be trusted to do the job right.

Right:

Lawn mowing and clean-up specialist. Can operate power equipment. Reasonable rates for expert and reliable work. Excellent references. Call Don Caswell, 555-1212.

Wrong:

Need job. Cut grass, clean-up, anything. Ask for Donny. 555-1212.

The same rules apply to writing a for sale ad. Make your readers feel that this is the best buy in a bike or a used canoe they have ever seen. Provide as much information as you can. Don't make readers guess about details they want to know about—especially the condition of the bike and how much you are charging.

Right:

Raleigh 10-speed bike, 22-inch frame. Used only two years. Like new condition. Asking $85. Call 555-1212.

Wrong:

Bike for sale. Make me an offer. Call Mike 555-1212.

HAPPY ADS – DISPLAY ADS

Classified ads are also used for public announcements. There is often a section for special birthdays or congratulations. People love to have their birthdays announced, and it's nice to congratulate people on special occasions. Congratulations may be for a graduation, for someone's wedding anniversary, or for any other notable achievement you want to broadcast to the world.

Large ads, especially those that use pictures, are called "display ads." You will find a space for a display ad on the back page. Use this space to advertise anything you want to sell. Describe the item, tell why it's a bargain, draw a picture of it, and be sure to tell the price of the article. Don't forget to use lots of color in your advertisement.

Hey, Newsnose! What does the word "classifieds" mean?

This is short for "classified advertisements." The short ads in the classified section are sorted by their "class": help wanted, places to rent, homes for sale, articles for sale, pets, services, and so on. Nearly everyone is looking for something: a job, a pet, a bike that doesn't cost too much, or a bargain in a used car. If you need something, if you want to get rid of something, or if you want to tell the world about something— use the classifieds.

The Book & Movie REPORTER

- Editor's Choice Book Review
- Designer Book Jacket
- Books and the World
- Favorite Book List
- Golden Flashlight Award

A Book Review

EDITOR'S CHOICE BOOK REVIEW

When you do a book review, you are your newspaper's book critic. You tell a little bit about a book you have read and why you liked it or why you didn't like it. Remember—your readers are actually more interested in the WHY of your opinion than in the opinion itself.

When you tell what the book is about, tell just a little bit—not enough to spoil your readers' fun. A good place to start is with the setting—that is, where the book takes place and when. For example, *The Hound of the Baskervilles* takes place in England during the 19th century. The story is played out in an English home and the surrounding countryside of mysterious fields and swamps.

Then, give just a general idea of what the book is about. Say something like this: "The story tells how detective Sherlock Holmes solves the mystery of why a large dog is terrorizing the Baskerville family."

The characters are important to the enjoyment of a story, too, so they should be mentioned. For example, you can tell what role the characters play in the story: the captain of a pirate ship, a woman who owns a ranch, an old sheep dog, a comical rabbit.

DESIGNER BOOK JACKET

A picture of the book you review will make the page more interesting and more colorful. You can copy a picture from the book or its cover, or you can draw your own picture.

WORTH QUOTING

Find something that is said in the book that you would like to share with your readers. This can be serious or funny, heart warming or exciting. A good quote can often make a person want to read the book.

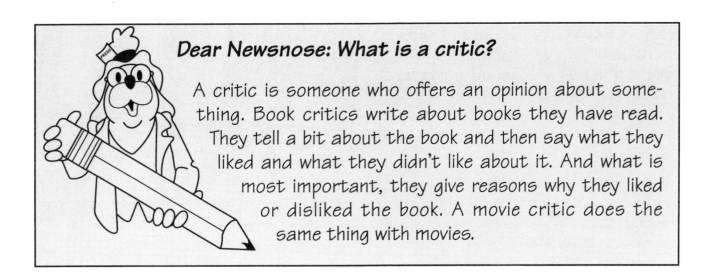

Dear Newsnose: What is a critic?

A critic is someone who offers an opinion about something. Book critics write about books they have read. They tell a bit about the book and then say what they liked and what they didn't like about it. And what is most important, they give reasons why they liked or disliked the book. A movie critic does the same thing with movies.

The Book Bag

READ A BOOK, SEE THE WORLD

When you write this article you will be telling about a story you have read that takes place somewhere besides in your own neighborhood. Tell the time when the story takes place. Then tell about the places you have been to in the book, and about the people you have met there.

BOOKS ABOUT . . .

What is your favorite subject, topic or hobby? Whatever it is, you can be sure there is a book about it. Let's say you are a baseball nut. You read anything and everything you can find about baseball. Head the column "Books About Baseball." Then make a list of books and their authors that talk about baseball.

One of the best ways to find the titles of lots of books about your favorite subject is to visit the library. Ask the librarian to show you where books on this subject are kept. Or, ask the librarian to show you how to find the names of these books in the library's card catalog or computer.

THE GOLDEN FLASHLIGHT AWARD

There are some books that are so exciting you can't put them down once you start reading. So when you go to bed, instead of going to sleep like you're supposed to, you take your book under the covers and read by flashlight. That way no one sees the light shining under the door.

Write down the title and author of a book that was so good it kept you up most of the night reading this way.

Tell me, Newsnose . . . How can you see the world by reading a book?

Imagination is how—through your imagination and the imagination of the author. Stories are set all over the world. So when the author puts a story in India, it's very much like getting a view of India.

You can travel in time, too. Lots of books describe what the future might be like. And other books are set hundreds and even thousands of years in the past. Some books are set in imaginary and fantastic places that no one can ever see except by reading about them.

Show Time

MOVIE SPECTACULAR

Here is a chance to be a critic again. But remember, critics don't just tell what they like or don't like about a movie. A movie critic tells something about the movie first—who's in it, what it's about—and then provides reasons for liking certain things and disliking others. Write your story as if you are discussing the movie with a friend.

Be sure you have a pad and pencil in hand as you watch the movie you are going to review in your newspaper. Give the viewing your entire attention. Make notes about it. You will want to catch and remember things about the movie that you may ordinarily ignore when you watch just for fun.

VIDEO ADVICE

There are two things you can talk about here. You can review a program you have seen on TV, or you can tell what you think about a video tape you bought or rented. Your opinion counts. It helps your readers decide if they will be interested in the video you have described.

Once again, you will want to have a pad and pencil handy to make notes. Watch the credits before and after the show to see who's in it, and who wrote and directed it. This is information your readers want to know. Jot down where the action takes place—New York, California, Paris. If there's a funny line to tell your readers about, write that down so you can quote it accurately. You may not use all the things you write down, but you will want a lot to pick and choose from as you begin writing.

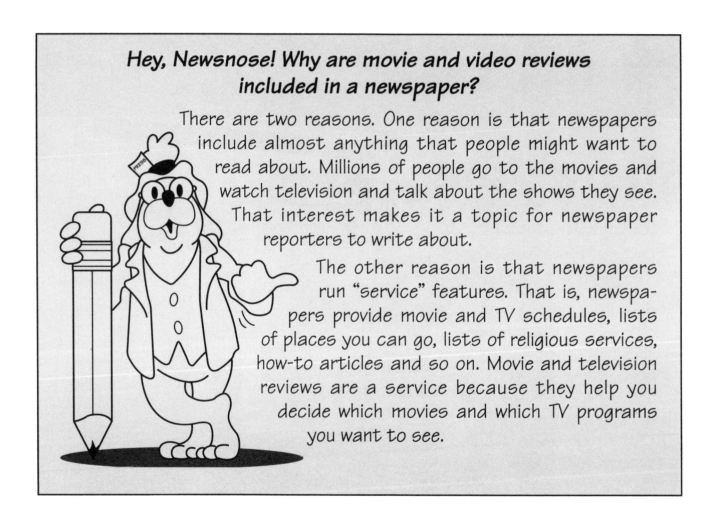

Hey, Newsnose! Why are movie and video reviews included in a newspaper?

There are two reasons. One reason is that newspapers include almost anything that people might want to read about. Millions of people go to the movies and watch television and talk about the shows they see. That interest makes it a topic for newspaper reporters to write about.

The other reason is that newspapers run "service" features. That is, newspapers provide movie and TV schedules, lists of places you can go, lists of religious services, how-to articles and so on. Movie and television reviews are a service because they help you decide which movies and which TV programs you want to see.

Star Stuff
LOOKING AT THE STARS

This is the place to talk about the stars. If you are a special fan of a particular star, you probably know enough about him or her to write a story. But the best way to write about a star is to do some research.

You can find many articles about currently popular stars in movie and TV magazines, *People* magazine, *Parade, TV Guide*, newspapers and general magazines.

If you want to write about a star of yesteryear, you are likely to find books in the library that will give you all the information you need. Ask the librarian for help if you need it.

If you want to write to a star to get personal information, there are encyclopedias in the library that tell about famous living people. Most of the time they will give you an address where you can send your letter. Ask your librarian to show you these books and how to use them.

If a star is appearing in your city, phone the theater or auditorium and see if you can get an interview. It may work and it may not. That's what happens with reporters. Sometimes they get lucky, and sometimes they don't.

NOW PLAYING

List the movies playing in town. Or, make a list of the best movies playing on cable TV. Use your local newspaper to check the times and places.

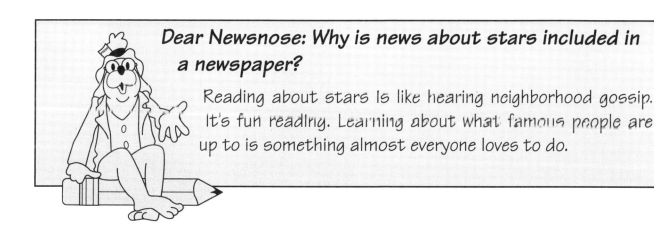

Dear Newsnose: Why is news about stars included in a newspaper?

Reading about stars is like hearing neighborhood gossip. It's fun reading. Learning about what famous people are up to is something almost everyone loves to do.

The Travel REPORTER

Around the World
The Traveler's Guide
People and Places
Hometown Trivia
Going Places
Along the Way
Special Correspondent

The Front Page

AROUND THE WORLD

Write about any place you want to write about that you think your readers will find interesting. This can be anywhere you have been, or anywhere you would like to go.

Once you have chosen the place, use Newsnose's tips to find out as much as you can about it. You can't tell everything there is to know about a place. So just hit a few highlights: the people, beautiful places to visit, the things you can do there.

Notice that the column begins with the words WITH and DATELINE. "Around the World With . . ." can be you, or it can be the name of the person who provided the information you are using.

A "dateline" tells the name of the place you are writing from. (Pretend you are writing from the place you are writing about.) It also gives the date when you wrote the article. Example: Cairo, May 11, 1993.

Use the picture box to illustrate your story. You can paste in a picture from a travel brochure, a newspaper, or a magazine, or you can use a photo you took on a trip. You can also draw your own picture if you want to.

THE TRAVELER'S GUIDE

This calls for a thumbnail sketch of the place you have written about in your main travel article. Fill in the name of the capital city if the article is about a country, state, or province. If you have written about a county, parish, or city—use the name of the most important place you know about.

Some interesting things to include in your guide are: the size of the place, how many people there are (a lot or a few), the name of the leader or a local important person, and the language spoken. Then make any other comments you think would be interesting or useful for your readers to know about.

Newsnose, please . . . if I've never been around the world, how can I write about it?

Check out the travel section in your library. Read the travel section of your local newspaper. Find a travel magazine or travel brochures in the library. Watch a TV show about a foreign country and make notes. Write to the embassy of a country that interests you and ask them to send information. (Where can you find the address? In the library, of course.)

Hometown News and Views

PEOPLE AND PLACES

People from the east often like to take their vacation in the west. People from the north go south. Those from the south go north. Americans go to Europe and Europeans go to America.

So the chances are good that somebody from somewhere else is going to want to visit your town. Here is your chance to tell others why your town is an interesting place to visit.

If your town has 110 people and 475 cows, you might feel like writing, "Well, that's it folks." Or, if you live in a big town, you might be tempted to say, "Aaah, nothing ever happens here."

All this means is that you have to dig into your imagination a little. If there are 475 cows, you could say that this is a great place to enjoy the quiet of the country. The mountains or desert or lakes nearby may be a welcome resting spot for visitors. There may be some interesting history attached to the town.

Get acquainted with your town and write about it with love. And whatever you talk about, don't forget to include a picture in the picture box.

HOMETOWN TRIVIA

Ask a question about your town and then amaze your readers with the answer you write on the back page of the travel section.

How tall is Middleville's tallest skyscraper?
(Answer: Three stories. Sorry, that's the best we can do.)

When was the city of Fieldberg founded?
(Answer: 1821)

Your trivia question and answer can be funny or serious. There is some interesting little tidbit to write about in every town.

Aren't you a bit mixed up, Newsnose? How can I write a travel article about where I live?

Some of your readers may not live in your town, but would like to know about it. You are the best person to tell them about your town and what to see when they come for a visit.

On the Road

GOING PLACES

If your readers want to go to one of the places you have described in your travel articles, they want to know how to get there. They also want to know what there is to see and what there is to do once they arrive. If you have been to the place you are writing about, you can probably remember how you got there and what you did for fun.

You want your information to be accurate, however. So check with the maps and brochures Newsnose suggests you use to be sure of your facts.

Once you have your information, writing the article is a cinch. (By the way, this applies to all of your writing. If you do your research and get your information organized first, the writing is a piece of cake.)

The picture box can be used for a picture of the place you are writing about, or you can draw a map to show how to get there. If showing how to get there is too complicated (like the Takla Makam Desert in northwestern China, where the last 1,000 miles of the journey is by camel cart), just draw a map that shows the part of the world where this great place is located. Use a map, atlas, or a globe of the world if you need help.

ALONG THE WAY

This is the place to make a list of "must see" things along the way:

Stop at the Last Chance Cafe, where they serve cactus needles in a sauce made with rattlesnake milk.

Be sure to visit Deaf Echo Canyon. When you shout your name, the echo says, "What?"

And don't forget to create a colorful advertisement for the place you are writing about.

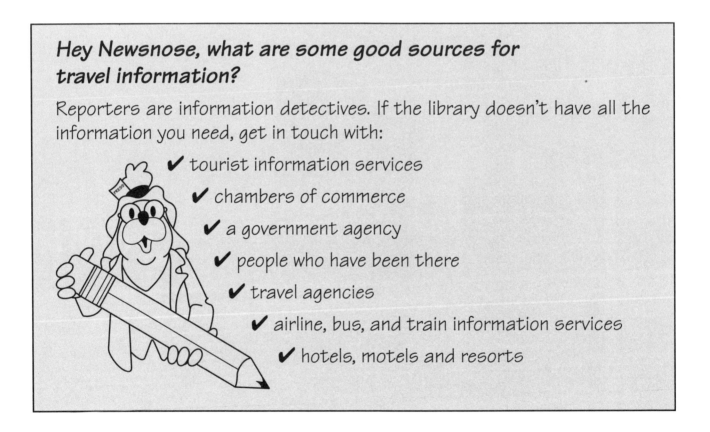

Hey Newsnose, what are some good sources for travel information?

Reporters are information detectives. If the library doesn't have all the information you need, get in touch with:

- ✔ tourist information services
- ✔ chambers of commerce
- ✔ a government agency
- ✔ people who have been there
- ✔ travel agencies
- ✔ airline, bus, and train information services
- ✔ hotels, motels and resorts

Special Correspondent

Imagine yourself someplace. This place can be a diamond mine in Africa or your Uncle Rutherford's chicken ranch in New Jersey. Then write a letter home telling about the place and what you are doing there.

In order to do this, of course, you will have to have some idea what it is like in a diamond mine, or on Uncle Rutherford's ranch. If you haven't been to these places you have to: 1) Use the old imagination again, and 2) Make another trip to your information sources in the library.

THE PICTURE BOXES

Special correspondents always take pictures. If you have written your letter from a place you have been to and where you have taken pictures, use one or two of these pictures in the picture boxes. If it's a place you have just imagined you have visited, try to find pictures of the place in a magazine or travel brochure. Cut them out and paste them in the boxes.

Special Correspondent

Say, Newsnose. What is a correspondent?

You are, for one. A correspondent is someone who sends information to another person. As a reporter and editor, that makes you a correspondent. A letter writer is also called a correspondent. A special correspondent is someone who has been sent to a special place to provide some special kind of information—as in: "We have sent a special correspondent to Peru to write a report about llama tails. We expect he will be a little behind in his observations."

The Sports REPORTER

Headline Sports
Box Scores
The School Beat
Around Town
College and the Pros
Champion of the Month
Fun with Sports

Headline Sports

THE BIG STORY

People do their best writing when they know what they're talking about. So the best choice for your big story is a sport you are interested in and know well. But even if you think you are an expert in your sport, you will still want to check your facts before you write your story.

For instance, you may want to write a story about a basketball game. Take notes as you watch the game. If you can, get a program that has the names of the players and notes about them. If it's a school game you may be able to interview the coaches and some of the players. If it's a game you watch on television, make notes as you watch, and then check your local newspaper the next day to pick up information and statistics you may have missed.

Research is often important when writing a story. You may have to check a player's record in the newspaper or in an almanac. If you are writing about a team at your school, records may be available in your school library or from the Phys. Ed. department.

There are many kinds of big sports stories you can write besides reporting the results of a game. The big story may be about why your favorite team is winning or losing this year. Fights among players would make interesting reading for your fans, or there may be problems with coaches and owners of teams that your readers will want to know about. Predictions about winners and losers for the coming season, along with the reasons for your predictions, always make good reading, too.

BOX SCORE

Use the box score either to show the statistics of a game you told about in your big story, or use it to show team and player standings in a sport. You can find examples of box scores for pro or college sports in your local newspaper. World almanacs, sports almanacs and sports magazines are other good sources for box scores.

Hey, Newsnose! Is sports writing different from other kinds of writing?

In a word, YES. Sports writing is more punchy and tries to sound as exciting as the sports themselves. Headlines say things like "Green Wave Stuns Cathedral" for a big win and "Skins Edge Frontier" to describe a close game.

In the stories themselves there are hundreds of ways to say a team won or lost. Here are some of them: creamed, rolled over, dropped, stung, edged out, a squeaker, fell, were squashed by. You get the idea.

A football team doesn't just move the ball, they march or drive or power their way. Before you write your own sports story, read the sports pages of your local newspaper to see how the pros write.

Where the Action Is

THE SCHOOL BEAT

The sports closest to your readers' hearts are the ones they are closest to—school sports. School sports are also the sports you know most about. You probably know many of the athletes and the coaches. You may even play on one of the teams. All of this is what newspaper reporters call "access." This means that the firsthand sources for your stories are easily available to you.

The three ways to gather information for a sports story (or any story, for that matter) are: *observe*, *read*, and *listen*.

You observe when you watch a game. Make notes as you observe.

You read when you do research. Sports research (and research for most other stories) can be done with books, newspapers, magazines, encyclopedias and almanacs. The sports department at your school can probably show you team records from previous years if you need them for your story.

You listen when you do an interview and when you discuss a sports situation with someone. Plan and prepare your questions ahead of time. Then listen carefully. Make notes during your discussion or get it on tape with a tape recorder. If you use a tape recorder you will want to make notes of important points as you replay the tape.

COLLEGE AND THE PROS

Here is where you may want to do some serious research as you write your story. If you are lucky enough to be able to attend a college or professional game in your area, make notes as you watch the game (observe). Use the program and information shown on the scoreboard at the game for notes for your story. And you may also want to report about the crowd, the food, the band and the cheerleaders. This is called "background" or "atmosphere" and can be interesting reading for people who weren't at the game.

You can also report on a game you watch on television. If you do this, use your newspaper to get information about the players and what is at stake in the game (a contest for first place, perhaps). As you watch, make careful notes of the statistics that are flashed on the screen. Also listen carefully to the sportscasters and write down information they provide that may help you write your story.

AROUND TOWN

Sports around town are as easy to report as sports at school, except that you may have to do a little more traveling to get your story. Sports around town include personal or team play for either kids or adults—baseball, hockey, events at the local "Y," bike races, marathons, golf, and so on.

If street or playground games are popular in your neighborhood, you can report on anything from stickball to handball to skateboarding. Your own personal sports program can also be turned into a story. If you do gymnastics, aerobics, jog, roller skate, bike, hike, hunt, fish, or just walk the dog—these are all sources for news of sports around town.

ON DECK

Make a list in this box of any upcoming sports events that your readers may want to know about. Or, you can list follow-up games in a sport that you told about in one of your "Where the Action Is" stories. Scheduled play-off or championship games are of special interest to sports fans.

Dear Newsnose: What is a beat?

A beat is a regular assignment that a reporter covers. A reporter who goes to police headquarters every day to see what the crime situation is, covers the police beat, or the crime beat. A reporter who covers schools has the school beat. A reporter who covers local politics has the city hall beat, and so on. When you are writing about local sports, you have the sports beat.

Profile

CHAMPION OF THE MONTH

Here is where you zero in on a particular athlete. After you have named the athlete you are going to write about, think for a moment about what you want to say. You can't include everything about this person in your story from the day he was born, so try to think of one special thing you want to concentrate on. This is called a focus for your story.

The athlete's won-loss record might be your focus. Perhaps you want to talk about what a nice person this athlete is. Or, the athlete may have achieved a lot in a short time. Perhaps your athlete may be a defensive tackle who terrorizes quarterbacks. There are many ways to approach and develop a story.

The prompts at the top of the Champion of the Month column are there to help give you ideas for a focus for your story. But you don't have to use them if you don't want to. The story may be done as an interview, or written from information you have read about the athlete.

Don't forget to illustrate your story. A picture of the athlete the story is about would be best. But if you can't find one, a general picture of a football game would work for a football player. A picture of the start of a marathon race would work well for a story about a runner. Cut these pictures from a newspaper or magazine.

CAREER HIGHLIGHTS

Use this box to summarize the most outstanding things the athlete has done. You may have to search for these facts in newspaper and magazine stories, or in a sports almanac.

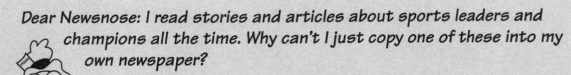

Dear Newsnose: I read stories and articles about sports leaders and champions all the time. Why can't I just copy one of these into my own newspaper?

You can do that if you want to. It's an easy way to get a story. But you won't have the same pride in what you have done that you have when you write the story yourself.

In the world of newspapering, and in other kinds of writing as well, copying someone else's work is called plagiarism (play' jer ism). Writers who copy can be sued in court. Editors usually fire a reporter who is caught copying. In school, teachers and principals may take severe action against students who copy.

Fun With Sports

SPORTS BLOOPER

Just about everyone knows about some dumb play, a fluke, or an embarrassing moment in sports. Here's your chance to tell the funny story. It may have happened to you, you may have seen it happen, or you may have seen an especially funny blooper on TV or in a video.

If you can't think of anything funny that really happened, use your imagination. Make up a funny sports situation. You might start this kind of an article by saying, "Wouldn't it be funny if . . ." or "What do you suppose would happen if . . ." These expressions show your readers you are making up a story rather than reporting something that really happened.

Take your time writing this funny piece. Humor is harder to write than you might

think. Write your article several times, changing and correcting as you go, before putting it into your Sports Reporter newspaper. Don't forget to use the picture box to illustrate your story.

JOCK AND JILL

This is a funny situation that has been set up for you by a cartoonist. All you have to do is fill in the word ballons to create a funny sports comic strip. But, once again, try several gags before you put the best one into your comic strip.

TRIVIA, HISTORY, AND THE CRYSTAL BALL

Sports Trivia

All of the items on the fun page are fillers—interesting little tidbits that are easy and fun to read.

Sports enthusiasts are usually full of facts and statistics about their favorite game. It may seem dull fare to some people, but it's the cookies and ice cream of sports to die-hard fans.

You may remember that back at the beginning of this book, you saw that an old definition of news was given as something that makes a reader say "Wow! or "Gee whiz!"

Think up some bit of information about your favorite sport that will make other fans say "Wow!" or "Gee whiz!" or "Hey! Isn't that interesting."

Sports History

Sports history is another grabber for most readers. If you can't think of an interesting historical fact from your own store of knowledge—head for the library. Check sports books and almanacs to find an interesting fact for your readers. It's important to check your facts, even for little fillers. Your readers should be able to trust you as an honest writer and reporter.

The Crystal Ball

Just about everybody likes to make and read predictions—especially sports fans. And the reason that predictions make interesting reading is that your readers will probably disagree with you. This can start a good argument. And people love to have arguments about sports.

Why a fun page, Newsnose? I thought writing and newspapers were supposed to be all serious stuff.

There are all kinds of moods in writing, just as there are all kinds of moods when you talk to a friend. Sometimes you are serious and sometimes you joke around. Newspapers have lots of features that are on the light side: comics, cartoons, humor columns, and so on. Even serious articles sometimes have a bit of humor in them to make them easier to read.

Getting into the Newspaper Game

News Reporting as a Career

So you want to be a reporter . . .

If you think you want to be a reporter, there are questions you should ask yourself that can tell you if you really have the urge. You should be able to answer "yes" to all of the questions.

• Do I like to write stories and articles for others to read?

You should like to communicate with people. That is, you should feel it's important for you to pass your knowledge, ideas, and feelings along to others. And you should want to do this at least as much with written words as you do by talking.

• Am I curious and imaginative?

Reporters have to be a bit nosy. They need to be able to become interested in anything and everything they see or hear about. Reporters don't just write exciting stories about wars, fires, and crimes. They have to be curious about how governments work, how sewers are built, what's happening in the stock market, what's new in science and industry, and so on. They have to use their imaginations to be able to see what's interesting in the whole world, not just in parts of it.

• *Am I a good observer and a good listener?*

Reporters listen carefully. They want to hear what others have to say. They watch the world with interest. They not only *look* at the things they see, they *think* about them.

• *Can I be enthusiastic about my job?*

Reporters work on their own most of the time. So you have to be a person who can work without always being told what to do and when to do it. You have to like what you are doing and be willing to work long, sometimes boring hours in pursuit of a story.

• *Can I complete work on time?*

Reporters work against deadlines. A newspaper or a news broadcast has to operate on a strict schedule whether your story is ready or not. This means you have to be able to write quickly and accurately at the same time.

The importance of being a reporter

Joseph Pulitzer—one of the great newspaper owners and editors of all time—had this to say about the importance of journalism:

"Our Republic and its press will rise and fall together."

Pulitzer was suggesting that a country is as good, or as bad, as its newspapers. He said this at the beginning of the twentieth century, and if he were alive today, he would probably include television and radio news in his remarks.

Why is the press so important? Very few people are in a position to keep an eye on what is happening in government, business, and in the world in general. It is up to a good, honest and free press to be the watchdog that does this for us. It all starts with smart, hard-working reporters.

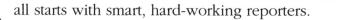

What you have to do to become a reporter

Nearly all reporters today are college graduates. Most of them major in writing in one way or another. Many are graduates of journalism schools in universities, but others are English, fine arts, history, or political science majors.

You will want to prepare yourself in high school by taking as many English, history and writing classes as you can. If there is a school newspaper or journalism course, get involved in these.

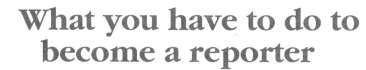

Journalism, and professional writing in general, is not highly paid work compared to other jobs that call for the same amount of education. So you had better like what you are doing. Writing has a certain amount of glamour and excitement to it, however, that make writers love their work so much that they wouldn't do anything else.

Steps in the Writing Process

There is writing . . . and then again, there is writing. There are as many ways to write as there are to talk.

A teacher speaks one way to a class and another way when coaching a football team. A politician speaks one way to an audience, another way to his family, and still another way to a newspaper reporter. You speak differently to your parents than you do to your friends.

Writing articles for others to read in a newspaper is different from the writing you do when you write a letter to a friend. It is also different from the writing you do for an examination in school.

No matter what they write, however, nearly all professional writers go through a procedure that is worth looking at. This procedure is not a set of rules that you must follow in order to be a writer. It is simply a series of steps that makes writing easier, and that produces better stories and articles for your readers. Not all writers use all of the steps in the procedure in exactly the same way. But they do use many of the steps, most of the time. They are worth looking at and remembering.

1. Keep a Journal

A journal is a book of thoughts and observations. It is a great mish-mash of things. It can be like a diary that records your ideas and feelings about things you have done and people you have met. It can contain snippets from conversations or articles you have heard or read somewhere. It can contain great ideas that come to you about solving big problems and little problems.

A journal does two things for a writer: 1) It keeps you writing every day. 2) It becomes a valuable source for ideas for stories, articles and even whole books that you may write someday.

2. Plug in to an Idea Factory

Sometimes reporters are given a subject to write about. Other times they are simply told to write something interesting that will fill two columns on the second page. Then they have to plug in to the idea factory.

Your journal will help. This is filled with your ideas. Then, look around you. Browse in the library. Ask yourself what you are really interested in and what things you know about. Make a list as ideas start coming. This is a kind of brainstorming. You can do it alone or with a friend.

3. Choose and Narrow Down Your Subject

Once you have an idea for something to write about, it has to be narrowed down. "Write a nature article," you are told. You are a bird lover, so you decide your article will be about birds. What birds? Okay—bluebirds. What about bluebirds? You get the idea. Whole books have been written about bluebirds! Perhaps, in the end, you decide to write only about how to attract bluebirds to your back yard. This would be an article with a very narrow focus. Always narrow the focus of your writing. This keeps you from wandering all over the place as you write, and it makes writing much easier.

4. Plan Your Writing

There is very little you can do in this world without doing some thinking and planning first. Going camping? Got to make plans. Going to a dance? Got to figure out what to wear, who to take, how to get there and how to get home again.

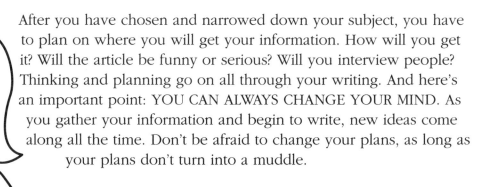

After you have chosen and narrowed down your subject, you have to plan on where you will get your information. How will you get it? Will the article be funny or serious? Will you interview people? Thinking and planning go on all through your writing. And here's an important point: YOU CAN ALWAYS CHANGE YOUR MIND. As you gather your information and begin to write, new ideas come along all the time. Don't be afraid to change your plans, as long as your plans don't turn into a muddle.

5. Gather Information

Sometimes this is called research. If you are writing about baseball, you will probably want to look at a baseball almanac or encyclopedia. You may want to check some old newspapers. You may want to interview a coach or a player.

Information is gathered in three ways: by reading, by observing, and by listening. And no matter how you gather it, your information should be kept in a pile of notes that keeps getting bigger and bigger and bigger. . . . until you are really ready to write.

6. Organize Your Information

The pile of notes you have will be a hodgepodge. This will have to be organized into what is useful for your narrowed-down subject and what is not. You will want to figure out what you might write about first, second and third.

Your organizing will eventually take the form of a written list of facts and ideas. Some writers turn this into an outline. Once again—it can't be said too often—YOU CAN ALWAYS CHANGE YOUR MIND! Don't follow a plan or an outline out the window if it doesn't seem to be working. If you change your plans you may have to start all over again. But what the heck! You *like* writing!

7. Write a Lead

This is not lead as in lead pipe, but lead as in lead the parade. You want something that will lead your writing—start it off, point a direction, and keep it moving. The best newspaper reporters say they spend more time writing a lead than they do writing the whole story. This is because once you have a lead that you like, the rest of the story just seems to flow from it.

A lead may be a dramatic fact: "A Boeing 727 collided with a small plane over San Diego and crashed, killing all 257 people on board." That will grab your readers and at the same time will give a direction to your writing.

"I will cry a hundred years from now when I think of what this wind did to my city and its people." This was the lead for a prize-winning newspaper story written after a tornado hit a midwestern city. It sets the tone for the story (an emotional one) and it creates a bond between the writer and the readers.

8. Writing a Rough Draft

This is your first attempt at writing your story or article. Many writers call this their sloppy copy. It's your first effort to get it all down on paper. You make changes, cross out, write in the margins. Make a mess. But get it down.

If you try to make your first draft your final one, you will be so hung up on getting it perfect that you won't be able to get your ideas on paper. Your smooth, well written article will come later.

9. Editing

Editing is the process of reading, correcting and changing your rough draft until you finally get your story just the way you want it. Sometimes this means tossing out the whole thing. But by writing a rough draft you have seen where you want to go, and the second effort will be better and easier to write.

Editing time is also the time to check spelling and grammar. If you aren't sure, look it up or ask someone who knows. Writers are always showing their work to others and saying: What do you think of this? Is this right? Writers depend on good editors to make their writing better. And writers write good stories by being very tough editors themselves.

10. Rewriting

This is the heartbreak hill of writing. It separates the pros from the also-rans. Writers have the biggest wastebaskets in the world—into which they toss story after story until they have one written the way they want it. If you have two weeks to write an article, you spend one week writing, and another week rewriting. If your two-week-old article is due on Monday morning and you start on Sunday night, it's goodbye rewrite and hello third-rate story.

If you think all this makes writing sound like a hard job, you're right! But good writers are good writers because they love what they do. And they get pleasure out of a story that is good because they worked hard at making it good.

One last word about getting to be a good writer: WRITE SOMETHING—ANYTHING—EVERY DAY. You become a good basketball player by playing. You become a good speaker by speaking. And you become a good writer by writing.

Good luck!

Glossary of Newspaper Words

Assignment
An event or story a reporter has been asked to write about.

Banner
A very large headline across a whole page.

Beat
A regular assignment for a reporter: city beat, police beat, etc.

Boldface type
Heavy, dark print that makes special words stand out.

Breaking news
A news event happening now.

Broadsheet
A full-size newspaper, as opposed to the smaller tabloid size.

Bureau
Newspapers have offices or bureaus in major cities around the world to cover news stories in these places.

By-line
The name of the writer at the beginning of a story.

Caption
The explanation that appears with a picture or drawing.

Cartoon balloon
The round design that points to a character's mouth and contains the words being spoken.

Cartoonist
An artist who draws comics or political cartoons.

City desk, city room
The office where local news is assigned, received, and edited.

Columnist
A person who writes a regular article, usually on one subject — sports commentary, humor, advice, food, etc.

Copy
All written material produced by reporters.

Copy editor
The editor who makes corrections in copy and sometimes shortens an article to fit the newspaper space available; sometimes called a rewrite editor.

Copyright
The exclusive right of a writer, artist, or newspaper publisher to receive money earned from a story or pictures. This is sometimes indicated by this symbol: © with a date.

Credit
A credit line tells where a writer has gotten information that is included in an article—especially if it was taken from another writer's work.

Critic
Someone who writes reviews of new books, movies, television shows, music, etc.

Dateline
The place and date where an article originates.

Deadline
The time when an article must be presented to the newspaper for editing and printing.

Exclusive

An "exclusive" is a news story, article, or interview that is given to only one special reporter.

Flag

The name of the newspaper as presented in its special design on the front page of the newspaper.

Freelance

A writer, artist, or photographer who does work for a newspaper or magazine, but who is self-employed and is hired temporarily for a special assignment. Also called a "stringer."

Head, headline, sub-head

These are the large words at the beginning of an article that attract a reader's eye and tell what a story is about. A sub-head is a little smaller and explains the headline a bit more.

Lead

Pronounced *leed*. This is the first sentence or the first few sentences that draw a reader into an article. It is also a writer's way to find a direction for a story.

Masthead

A box containing information about the newspaper: its name, where it is published, the names of the owners, publishers and chief editors. The masthead is often on the second page of a newspaper or on the editorial page.

Newsprint

The paper a newspaper is printed on.

Newsroom

The busy office at a newspaper where news arrives and is edited for publication.

News services

These are companies that furnish news to newspapers. Some of the largest and best known are The Associated Press (AP), United Press International (UPI), Reuters, and Newhouse News Service. You can frequently spot these names at the beginning of articles in your local newspaper.

Press

A general term that refers to the news industry. Someone might say: "I called a press conference." This means reporters ("the press") have been called to be given a news story.

Publisher

A publisher is the person who runs the newspaper or the company that owns the newspaper.

Scoop

When a reporter is able to get an important story printed before anyone else, it is a "scoop."

Stringer

An independent reporter who is hired part-time or on a temporary basis to write a special story.

Syndicate

A news and feature syndicate is a company that supplies comics, columns, cartoons, and other features to newspapers.

Syndicated columnist or cartoonist

A writer or artist who has work distributed to many newspapers by a news syndicate.

Tabloid

A small newspaper, as compared to a broadsheet or full-size newspaper.